WELCOME TO

Solve the puzzle be[low to find out]
what you were crea[ted to do! Put]
corresponding spot[s ...]
made us!

Answer: made to magnify God

DAY 1: MAGNIFY GOD

THE BIG TRUTH: God created everything there is, and yet He still wants to spend time with me.

ZOOM IN: I am important to God.

BONUS VERSE: John 1:12

TODAY'S POINT: God sees me.

JESUS AND THE CHILDREN
John 1:1-3,12; Mark 10:13-16

One day, people brought their children to Jesus to ask Him to bless them. Jesus' helpers tried to stop the parents. Jesus got very angry with His disciples and told them to let the children come. Jesus took the children in His arms and blessed them.

MAGNIFIED REACTIONS!

Do you like surprises? First draw the face you make when you are surprised with something good. Then draw or write about the different reactions to the children who came to Jesus.

A GOOD SURPRISE

DISCIPLES' REACTION

JESUS' RESPONSE TO THE CHILDREN

JESUS' RESPONSE TO THE DISCIPLES

BACKYARD TREASURE HUNT

Find the words hidden in the grass that reveal ways you can spend time with God. Why is spending time with God important? Remember, God created everything there is, and yet He still wants to spend time with you! See if you can find all six ways.

DAY 2: MAGNIFY GOD'S CARE

THE BIG TRUTH: God keeps the whole universe going, and yet He still cares about what's happening to me.

ZOOM IN: I can trust God to take care of me.

BONUS VERSE: Deuteronomy 31:8b

TODAY'S POINT: God cares about me.

JESUS CALMED THE STORM
Mark 4:1,35-41

Jesus used a boat to cross a lake with His disciples. A huge windstorm started. The boat started to fill up with water. Jesus was in the back of the boat asleep. The disciples woke Him up asking for help, and Jesus stopped the storm. The disciples were amazed that the wind and sea obeyed Jesus.

WHAT I CARE ABOUT

PEOPLE	THINGS

HOW DOES HE DO IT?

God created everything and He keeps everything going. Look up the Bible verses and match them to something they describe that God makes happen. Put a star beside the item you think is the coolest to experience.

- PSALM 8:3
- SUN RISING
- STARS SPINNING
- JOB 38:12
- JONAH 1:4
- WAVES CRASHING
- ME WAKING UP
- MY HEART PUMPING BLOOD
- PSALM 89:9
- PSALM 3:5
- STORMS SURGING
- PSALM 139:13

Is it hard to remember that God is making all these things happen? Why?

DAY 3: MAGNIFY GOD'S LOVE

THE BIG TRUTH: God is not OK with sin, and yet He still loves sinners like me.

ZOOM IN: I can be confident God loves me.

BONUS VERSE: Romans 5:8

TODAY'S POINT: God loves me.

THE WOMAN AT THE WELL
John 4:1-42

Jesus talked to a Samaritan woman at a well. She recognized that Jesus was different. Jesus told her that He is God's promised Savior. The woman told other people in the town about Jesus, the Savior. Many Samaritans from that town believed in Jesus.

CREEPY CRAWLY CODE

What is sin? Solve the code to find out.

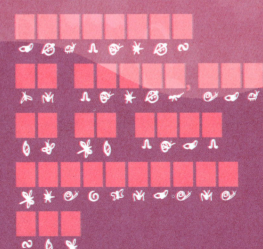

Answer: anything we think, say, or do that displeases God

REARRANGED RAINDROPS

When light hits tiny raindrops, it can make a giant rainbow with these colors: red, orange, yellow, green, blue, dark blue, and purple. Read the words next to each raindrop in this color order, then find the same promise in your Bible.

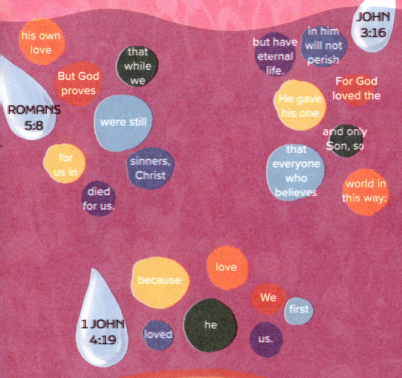

List some ways Jesus has shown you love.

PUDDLE PUZZLE

Drop in the correct letters to discover a marvelous thing Jesus did for you! Each pair of puddles will point you to the row and column where you can find the letter you need.

Answer: Jesus died on the cross as a substitute for anyone who believes.

J☐sus ☐☐☐☐ ☐☐☐☐ ☐☐☐☐ ☐☐☐☐ on th☐ cross ☐s ☐☐☐☐ subst☐tut☐ ☐or ☐☐☐☐ yo☐☐ who b☐l☐☐v☐s.

Do you want to know more about why Jesus died and came back to life? Check the last page in this booklet to learn more!

DAY 4: MAGNIFY GOD'S FORGIVENESS

THE BIG TRUTH: Jesus came to save the world, and that includes me.

ZOOM IN: I can trust Jesus as my Savior.

BONUS VERSE: John 3:16

TODAY'S POINT: God forgives me.

JESUS AND NICODEMUS
John 3:1-21, 18–20; 1 Corinthians 15:6

Nicodemus visited Jesus at night. Jesus taught Nicodemus about God's kingdom. Some time later, Jesus died on a cross. Nicodemus helped prepare Jesus' body to be buried. After three days, some women went to Jesus' tomb. It was empty! Jesus rose from the dead so that those who receive His gift of forgiveness can be part of God's family forever.

QUESTIONS FOR JESUS

If you could ask Jesus anything what would you ask Him?

_____

_____

_____

What do you think Nicodemus' questions revealed about his spiritual journey? Where are you in your journey with Jesus?

NEED FOR SEED!

Nicodemus was searching for answers to his questions. Looks like the birds made a mess searching for seeds. Can you find 12 words from the story summary on page 10 in the word search below?

```
J V Q X C Y A P V T A U G H T
M N P H Y R Y Y H U Z D C S N
T E H Y T K O R D C Q M E A M
N D W H W Y E S G A H Q Q R X
E I G M F E M T S K Z C T Y A
R I C G T O Q T Z O V J J L E
N Z D O G J R T Y K I J W A K
G N I I D A U G X N S U T I I
T Q F Y I E N K I Y I P O P N
A T T L N S M Y T V T M M U G
S U S E J W P U J Y E Z B X D
W O M E N M S V S M D N K Y O
O Q M B R H W P M L O N E A M
H W B S J O B R Q E S O I S T
S S Q D F Y T K M V L G Q M S
```

VISITED   KINGDOM   TOMB
THREE   NIGHT   GIFT
JESUS   TAUGHT   WOMEN
NICODEMUS CROSS   FORGIVENESS

DAY 5: MAGNIFY GOD'S FAITHFULNESS

THE BIG TRUTH: God is faithful with the big things in my life, and He will be faithful with the small things too.

ZOOM IN: I don't have to worry because God keeps His promises.

BONUS VERSE: Psalm 100:5

TODAY'S POINT: God keeps His promises.

JESUS TAUGHT ABOUT WORRY
Matthew 6:25-34

Jesus taught about what people should do when they worry. Jesus encouraged them to trust God. Jesus talked about the way God cares for everyday things like birds and flowers to help the people understand. The Bible is full of God's promises to provide what we need. God keeps His promises.

SCARE SCORE

Which activity would you worry about the most? Number them in order of scariest to least scary.

- ( ) Jumping off a 20-foot high dive
- ( ) Snow skiing down a mountain
- ( ) Riding a roller coaster that goes up to 120 miles per hour
- ( ) Swimming in water where you can't see the bottom
- ( ) White water rafting
- ( ) Going across a ropes course 30 feet in the air

MY TIME WITH GOD

God wants to spend time with you! You can spend time with Him in many different ways, but one way is reading your Bible. Read the verses below then answer the questions to help you start building a habit of spending time with God.

DAY 1

Read Mark 10:13-16. Things I noticed in this passage:

Questions I have:

Christ Connection: What does this story teach me about Jesus?

DAY 2

Read Mark 4:1,35-41. Things I noticed in this passage:

Questions I have:

Christ Connection: What does this story teach me about Jesus?

DAY 3

Read John 4:1-42. Things I noticed in this passage:

Questions I have:

Christ Connection: What does this story teach me about Jesus?

DAY 4

Read John 3:1-21. Things I noticed in this passage:

Questions I have:

Christ Connection: What does this story teach me about Jesus?

DAY 5

Read Matthew 6:25-34. Things I noticed in this passage:

Questions I have:

Christ Connection: What does this story teach me about Jesus?

EXPLORE GOD'S MAJESTY

Grab a Bible, a writing utensil, and a journal and keep reading! Divide up longer passages over several days if you need to.

After reading a passage, here are some questions you can ask to explore God's beauty and majesty more deeply.

1. What does this passage teach me about God?
2. What does this passage teach me about people?
3. What promises can be found in this passage?
4. What is this passage asking me to do, or change, in my life?

WEEK 1:
MAGNIFY GOD
- John **1:1-3,12**
- Genesis **1:1-25**
- Genesis **1:26-31**
- Psalm **139**

WEEK 2:
MAGNIFY GOD'S CARE
- Deuteronomy **31:8**
- Psalm **121:1-2**
- Psalm **23**
- 1 Peter **5:6-9**

WEEK 3:
MAGNIFY GOD'S LOVE
- Romans **5:8**
- 1 Corinthians **13:4-8,13**
- 1 John **3:1**
- Romans **8:37-39**

WEEK 4:
MAGNIFY GOD'S FORGIVENESS
- John **18–20**
- Matthew **6:14-15**
- Ephesians **4:32**
- Colossians **3:12-17**

WEEK 5:
MAGNIFY GOD'S FAITHFULNESS
- Psalm **100:5**
- Philippians **4:6-7,19**
- 2 Thessalonians **3:3**
- Hebrews **10:19-25**